How to Crochet for Beginners

Beginners

A Complete Step-by-Step Guidebook

Copyright © 2020

All rights reserved.

DEDICATION

Contents

Introduction

So, you want to learn how to crochet but aren't quite sure how or where to start? Have no fear - and welcome to the world of crochet!

If you're a beginner looking to start crochet, you'll find that it's very easy to get started as there is a wealth of information out there for you to peruse. To help you out, though, we've gathered some of our best and favorite tips and tricks here in this book to help you out.

Crocheting is an art that might seem awkward at first, but once you get the hang of holding on your crochet hook and working through a row of stitches, it will become second nature for you.

The delicate art of crocheting is a lifelong skill that you'll use to make beautiful gifts for others and items for your home and wardrobe. Start by learning a couple of basic stitches, and build on that with more advanced basic stitches. First, figure out what size and style hook feels most comfortable for you. Then, start with simple yarns and beginner patterns, and you'll be a pro in no time.

What Do You Need to Crochet

1. Crochet hook

You don't need many supplies to get started with crochet. The key item is the crochet hook, and there are plenty of different sizes and types. We suggest a size that's in the middle ranges, such as 4 mm through 6 mm. That's G/6 through J/10 in American terms.

When it comes to the best crochet hooks, it really depends on what you're crocheting and your personal preference (based on your hand shape and movements). Most people call these crochet hooks while others call them crochet needles. Whichever you prefer, there are several different types. Let's go over crochet hooks:

Steel: These crochet hook sizes (the right column) are the smallest hook sizes are usually reserved for fine thread crocheting, such as doilies.

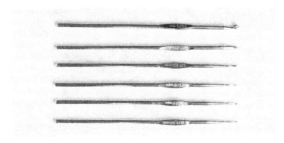

Aluminum: The most "generic" hook choice. Aluminum crochet hooks are available in a large range of sizes and is popular (especially for beginners) because the yarn glides smoothly.

Plastic: Popular choice and cost-effective. these are available in all sizes (even jumbo!).

Bamboo: Lightweight and warm in the hand; these crochet needles are available in all sizes except the smallest and jumbo sizes.

Wood: Besides bamboo, other wood is used to make crochet hooks as well. Wood can be in the standard shape or made with curves to be economic. Sometimes the wood is even colored to make the hook even more distinctive.

Tunisian: Also called a cro hook, these are longer than regular hooks and sometimes have a hook on the end. Like a knitting needle, you keep your stitches on a Tunisian crochet hook as you work. Tunisian crochet is also called afghan crochet.

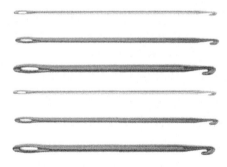

Ergonomic: Designed to reduce the strain in your hands as you crochet, these hooks usually have larger soft handles or handles you can insert a regular hook into.

The Knook: A long crochet hook with a hole running through one end. You thread a piece of yarn through the hole in the knook needle, and you can create stitches that look like knitting.

How to Hold a Crochet Hook

Holding a crochet hook with the pencil grip

There are plenty of different ways you could hold a crochet hook and yarn, but most of the time, crocheters fall into either of two groups: the pencil grippers and the knife grippers. Learn how each method works, as well as how to hold a Tunisian crochet hook.

As you try out these grips, keep in mind that these are only the most common ways of working. There are lots of possibilities and variations, so if they don't work for you, keep trying different things to see what's most comfortable for you.

The Pencil Grip

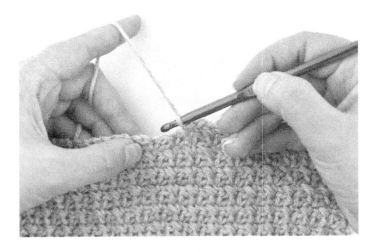

When you hold your crochet hook in much the same way you'd hold a pencil or pen, it's called the "pencil grip." The pencil grip gives you the same type of control as you would have when writing with a pencil or pen, or when painting with a paintbrush.

In this method, the hook typically works from above and goes down into the stitches.

To crochet with your hook pencil style, hold the crochet hook with the thumb, index finger, and middle finger of your right hand (see the left-handed version below). Hold your crochet work and regulate the yarn and yarn tension with your left hand. You can also use both hands to hold your crochet work with some of it in your left hand, and some held with your pinkie and fourth finger of your right hand.

Holding a crochet hook with the knife grip

When you use the "knife grip," it's similar to holding a dinner knife. This is an overhand grip that gives you the same type of control as you have when cutting your food with a knife.

Knife-grippers often claim that this method is the easiest on the hands; critics claim that it is less precise than the pencil grip. Even if you typically use the pencil grip, you may find the knife grip more comfortable when working with large hooks.

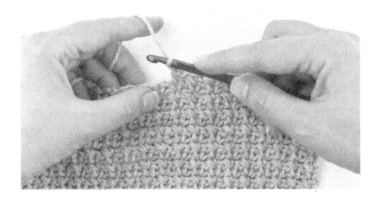

In this method, the hook typically works from below and goes up into the stitches.

To crochet with your hook knife-style, hold the crochet hook in your right hand with your hand over the hook and with your index finger slightly extended to guide the hook. Hold your crochet project in your left hand while regulating the yarn and the yarn tension.

How to hold a tunisian crochet hook

A Tunisian crochet hook (otherwise known as an afghan hook, or an afghan crochet hook) is different than a traditional crochet hook. These hooks are longer, and they don't have a thumb rest.

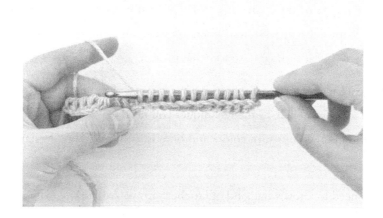

You don't want to use a pencil grip to hold a Tunisian crochet hook. Instead, use an overhand grip that allows you to manipulate both the hook and the work as you crochet. It's almost like a cross between a pencil and knife grip.

When working in Tunisian crochet, let your working hand form a loose, easy fist. The crochet hook needs to be able to rotate and move freely inside the hand. Use your fingers and hand for both manipulating the crochet hook and the work-in-progress, including scooting stitches further in one direction or the other on the hook.

2. Yarn

As a beginner, you may not want to use ultra expensive yarn, so we suggest a budget-friendly but crocheter favorite, such as Red Heart Super Saver.

There are plenty of different yarns for you to use for each of your crochet projects. With that said, different fibers of yarn will result in a different look depending on what yarn you use for what project.

There are a lot of things to keep in mind as you start learning how to crochet, from the tools you need, to the techniques you need to know. Before you can even get to choose your yarn colors and brands, you need to understand yarn weights.

You also need to know what kind of crochet yarn you're working with in order to choose the right hook size for the best outcome of your project. Once you've got the right tools for your project, you can start working on crocheting the perfect scarf, hat, or whatever you plan to make.

Hank vs Skein: Crochet Yarn Basics

I'm sure you're wondering how to choose the proper yarn for your crochet patterns. I don't blame you - there are SO many options! Well, let's start with the basics. Yarn can be called **a skein, a hank** or **a ball**. Most yarn that you'll buy at a bigger yarn or craft store will come in skeins or balls, while

A ball of yarn is yarn that's wrapped up in a ball, as the name suggests. It's round, and you can pull from within the ball or from the outside to start crocheting.

A skein of yarn is similar to a ball, except it is a more oval shape. You can still pull from within the skein to start crocheting or work from the outside end.

A hank of yarn is yarn that's been wound into a larger ring of yarn. It's then twisted to keep it from tangling. When you receive a hank of yarn, you'll need to wind it into a ball or skein before you start using it (or risk a tangled headache).

When first learning how to crochet I suggest you start out with cheap crochet yarn as you're probably going to make a lot of mistakes. You'll either leave the mistakes or you'll rip them out and start over, aka frog it (rip it, rip it).

Types of Crochet Yarn and Yarn Weight

As a beginner, I found it easiest to work with bulky weight yarn as it slid through my fingers easily. When working with bulky yarn, you also work with a larger hook size making the whole process a breeze. But should you buy acrylic yarn or still with heavy wool yarn? Maybe you should go with a silk blend?

When trying to decide on yarn, your first choice will be between natural fibers and synthetic. From there, you have a variety of options available to you.

Synthetic yarns are man-made and produced, but are often cheaper (though not always the softest), but they can usually handle machine washing and drying.

On the flip side, natural yarns like cotton or silk (or even a blend) tends to be of a higher quality. These fibers are naturally softer and more luxurious... but they might require more careful care.

When choosing the proper yarn for your crochet patterns you should also know the different yarn weights to choose from. Yarn weights play a crucial role when working up patterns. On every skein of yarn, you'll see what type of yarn it is and what the recommended hook size is. Using that yarn with the specified hook size will give you the best results.

What's the Best Crochet Yarn For...?

Though there are no hard and fast rules for choosing the best yarn for crochet projects, there are some factors to consider. You and your recipients will have personal preferences, such as picking natural or synthetics, thickness, colors, but I wanted to share some tips for choosing yarn for specific projects, which will help you narrow it down.

Best yarn for crochet socks? If you are making socks to wear around the house or during colder months, then you'll want a thicker yarn. A lighter, everyday pair of socks should use a thinner yarn or crochet thread. Other factors to consider with socks is that you will want a yarn that's absorbent and breathable. Cotton is a great choice but a cotton blend with some stretch is better since the pulling of socks requires flexibility.

Best yarn for crochet hats? Like socks, hats should use a stretchable yarn if it's a beanie or winter-type snug-fitting hat. Most hats use worsted weight or chunky because they are thicker. A wool blend adds the needed warmth. However, you need to consider any allergies since it will be in contact with skin. If it's not a hat needed for warmth, you can go with a lighter weight. Soft yarn is essential for hats since you don't want it to be uncomfortable!

Best yarn for crochet scarves? Before choosing the best yarn for scarves, ask a few questions: is this an indoor or outdoor scarf? Are you wanting to use multiple yarn colors, solid, or a variegated yarn type? Are there any allergies to consider? The answers to these questions will play a role in what you choose. Scarves can really be made of any yarn and no matter what you decide, you will find a pattern to use. Just make sure it's soft and whoever is wearing it will be happy!

Best yarn for crochet sweaters? Because sweaters are often pulled over the head, you will want there to be some flex in the yarn. However, if it's a cardigan or you want it to be structured and stay taut, then flexibility isn't going to be as important. Consider seasonality. A spring or summer sweater should be light and airy but a fall or winter sweater should be bulky or super bulky.

Best yarn for crochet blankets? Softness is the correct thickness is the most important factor in blankets. A large blanket can be expensive if you choose a high-quality yarn, so make sure you consider the full amount of yarn you need before starting. It's rare to use a yarn weight lighter than 4 because you want it to have the right amount of thickness (though baby blankets are an exception since they are small and need to be lightweight). Most yarn companies also have a line of blanket-specific yarns that are perfect for throws, afghans, and other similar crochet projects.

3. Scissors

Nothing too fancy here. A pair of your standard scissors will work. We do suggest that they are sharp enough to cut through the yarn cleanly. You don't want it to split because of a bad cut.

As you start crocheting more, there are other materials and tools that will come in handy but are optional. These include:

- Stitch/place markers
- Stitch counter
- Measuring tape/ruler
- Crochet gauge tool
- Yarn needle

One of the ways to get everything you need at the start is to purchase a beginner crochet kit. It will include everything you need besides the yarn and often comes complete with a handy carrying case.

How to Begin Crochet

When you are first starting off, start crochet with the basics. Start small and then work on working your way up. Begin by practicing all the basic stitches, from your initial slip stitch and foundation chain up through a double or treble crochet stitch.

There are so many crochet patterns that are made by these basic stitches, so you'll have a wide variety of projects to choose from.

1. Slip Knot

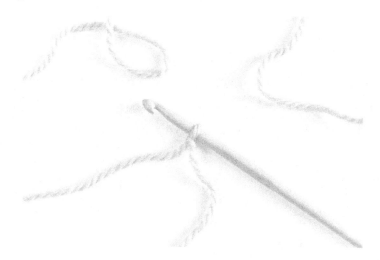

A slip knot is the first step in almost all crochet projects. There are multiple ways to create slip knots and this helpful guide shows one popular approach. It's a great choice for beginners who need to learn how to start their work.

Not only does this slip knot method form the knot you need to begin, but it also starts the rhythm and motion that carries on through the rest of your crochet.

How to Hold the Yarn

Grasp the yarn in your left hand, between your thumb and index finger, and allow the yarn to flow freely over your index finger. Support the yarn with your middle finger. The tail of yarn that's not connected to the ball of yarn should be in the front.

How to Hold the Crochet Hook

Grasp your hook in your right hand, using either a pencil grip or a knife grip (the photo shows a knife grip). Your fingers should be relaxed enough to move freely, but they should grip tightly enough to maintain precise control over the hook.

To start, keep the hook facing upward. Slip the crochet hook between your index finger and the yarn.

Twist the Yarn to Make a Loop

Use the crochet hook to lift the yarn above your non-dominant hand. Next, twist the yarn to form a loose loop on the hook. Essentially you are turning the hook in a circle.

This produces a twisted loop on the hook. It's not secure yet, but it is beginning to look like the start of a crochet project.

Wrap the Yarn Over the Hook

Hold the end tail of yarn between your middle finger and thumb. Use your index finger to manipulate the other end of the yarn as it unwinds from the ball. The yarn should loop over your index finger and then pass between your other fingers to create good tension.

Wrap the yarn over the crochet hook from behind and then over the top.

This may all feel a little awkward at first, but the more you practice, the more natural it feels. Before you know it, you'll be doing it without thinking.

Draw the Yarn Through the Loop

Use your crochet hook to draw the hooked yarn through the loop you created on the hook.

The yarn that you are working with comes through the loop and forms a loose slip knot.

Tighten Your Slip Knot

You should now have a loose slip knot on your crochet hook. Leave the knot on the crochet hook and pull gently on both ends of yarn to tighten it. Be careful not to over-tighten it, as the crochet hook should move easily inside this loop. It should be snug but not excessively tight.

Your first slip knot is finished and now you can begin your crochet project! The next step is to form your starting chain.

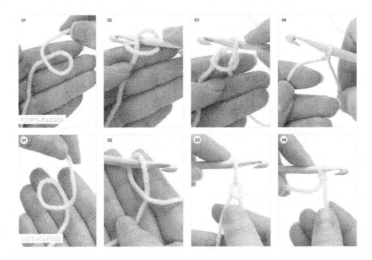

Tip. In crochet, the beginning slip knot is not usually counted as a stitch. This differs from knitting, where the first slip knot does create a stitch. This can be helpful when you are first looking at crochet patterns, which typically tell you how many stitches to begin within your foundation chain.

2. Chain Stitch

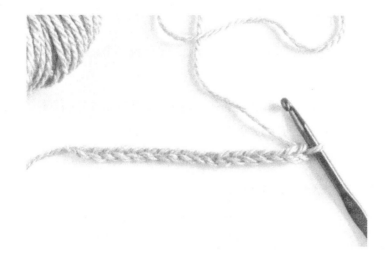

Chain stitches are an integral part of crocheting. Other than a slip knot, the first step in a project is usually to create a series of chain stitches. They are one of several essential stitches that every beginner should know.

Most crochet projects begin with chain stitches forming the foundation on which you build the rest of the project.

Beyond the foundation chain, crochet projects often contain chain stitches scattered throughout the rest of the pattern too. The chain stitches combine with other stitches to create the design and construction.

Keeping your tension correct for chain stitches can take some practice, but it's an easy stitch to learn and start your crochet.

First, form a slip knot.

With the slip knot on the crochet hook, grasp the knot with your left hand. The slip knot should face you.

The yarn coming from the ball should flow over your index finger. Use your other fingers and thumb to hold the working chain and keep the correct tension on the yarn as you crochet.

How to Hold the Crochet Hook

Grasp your crochet hook in your right hand using a pencil grip, knife grip, or whatever feels most comfortable to you.

To start, hold the crochet hook facing upwards. With each chain stitch that you crochet, rotate the hook by approximately one-quarter turn counterclockwise. It's okay to turn it more if you need to, but the goal is to make each move as precise and fluid as possible.

Yarning Over the First Chain Stitch

While your crochet hook is still inside the slip knot, loop the working yarn over the hook from back to front. Sometimes it helps to hold the slip knot in place on the hook with your right index finger.

Rotate your crochet hook by about one quarter turn counterclockwise as you loop the yarn to hook it.

Forming the First Chain Stitch

After you've hooked the yarn, draw it through the slip knot.

As you draw the yarn through, you will likely find it easier to complete the stitch if you return the hook to its original position facing upwards.

Crocheting More Chain Stitches

This is the first completed chain stitch.

To make another chain stitch, hook another loop and draw it through. Repeat this as many times as necessary. As you crochet, use your thumb and index finger to guide your newly formed chain stitches downward.

As you work, you'll find a rhythm in rotating the crochet hook as you hook the yarn and then rotating it back as you draw it through. This rhythm makes the process easier and faster.

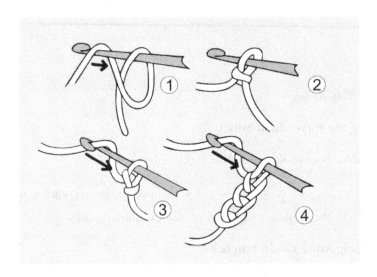

Tips for Making a Foundation Chain

- Count accurately: Typically the slip knot doesn't count in the number of chain stitches required in a pattern's foundation chain. Begin your count with the first chain stitch you make.

- Modify as needed: Everybody crochets a bit differently and there are many possible ways to hold the yarn and position the hook when crocheting a chain stitch. These instructions demonstrate one way of doing it. If this way is not comfortable for you, feel free to modify your way of working to suit your preferences.

- Maintain even tension: Practice until your chain stitches are smooth, even, and not too tight.

- Don't be afraid to change hooks: If you are crocheting with cotton or other non-stretchy yarn, it may be necessary to make your foundation chain using a crochet hook that is one size larger than the hook you plan to use for crocheting the rest of the project. If you find that your foundation chain is too tight in proportion to the first several rows of stitches that follow it, consider starting over using a larger hook for the chain. This is not always a necessity with resilient fibers such as wool, but it might be helpful, depending on the pattern you are using.

3. Single Crochet

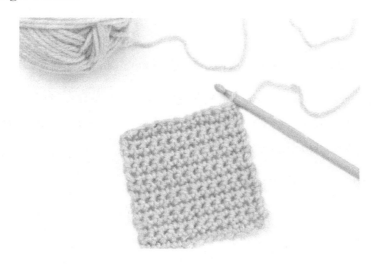

If you want to learn how to crochet, single crochet is one of the most important stitches you need to know. A majority of crochet patterns and projects incorporate single crochet stitches.

Single crochet (referred to as double crochet in British crochet patterns) is one of the easiest stitches to master. Once you've learned the single crochet stitch, there are infinite possible ways to use it. You can work it in rows, in rounds or spirals, as edging, in different parts of the stitch for different effects, and combined with other stitches in countless variations.

Insert Your Crochet Hook

After you form the foundation chain of stitches, insert the hook through the first chain. For the second row and beyond, insert your hook into the single crochet stitch directly below it in the row.

Slide the hook under both loops on the top of the chain.

Some patterns have you work through only one of the loops, which creates a different look–you can see samples at the end of this tutorial. When in doubt, go through both loops.

Yarn Over and Grab the Yarn

With the crochet hook in place, prepare to draw up a loop. Wrap the yarn over your crochet hook, and grab it with the hook.

When you've practiced these steps to the point that they are automatic, you might find that you get to the point when there isn't a gap between the first and the second steps. Your hook will grab the yarn just as soon as you insert it into the stitch.

Draw up the Loop

Pull or "draw" the hook and working yarn through the loops. You should now have two stitches or "loops" on your hook.

Yarn Over Again

Wrap the yarn around your crochet hook again, and hook the yarn.

Draw the Yarn Through Both Loops

Draw the hook and yarn through both of the loops on the hook. This completes the single crochet stitch. One loop remains on your crochet hook. This loop is the starting point for your next stitch.

You can repeat this sequence of steps as many times as needed to create additional single crochet stitches across the row (or round).

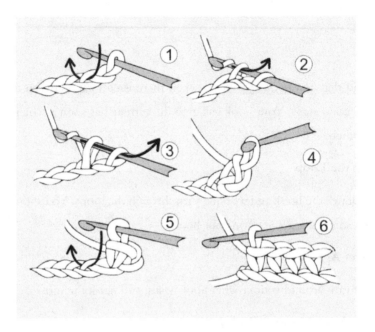

Tips for Beginners

If you are working your crochet in rows, the first row can be a challenge, especially for beginners. Many beginning crocheters have difficulty holding the work; at the beginning, there isn't much there to hold onto.

If you have trouble working your first row of single crochet stitch, ask an experienced crocheter to work the first several rows for you. Then you can continue crocheting on the same piece. After the first few rows are complete, you'll find it easier to hold the work.

After working enough rows to master the single crochet stitch, you'll have a much easier time working those tricky first rows in future projects.

4. Double Crochet

Double crochet is one of the essential basic crochet stitches. While you could crochet plenty of projects without it, the double crochet is a foundational crochet stitch that most people learn almost as soon as they begin crocheting.

Learning how to double crochet is important if you want to work most crochet patterns. You can use double crochet stitch on its own in rows and in the round. It's also useful for creating very common crochet stitch patterns, including the classic granny square and the popular v-stitch.

Wrap the Yarn Over the Crochet Hook

With one stitch on the hook, wrap the yarn over your crochet hook.

Insert Your Hook Where The Stitch Will Go

Insert your crochet hook into the stitch or space desired. If you're starting with a foundation chain, skip the three chains closest to the hook and insert the hook in the fourth chain.

Next, wrap the yarn over the crochet hook so that the hook part can grab the yarn.

As you wrap the yarn over, it's like wrapping the yarn over before you inserted the hook. The difference is that there's more yarn on your hook at this point so it's a little more difficult to maneuver. You'll soon get the hang of the motion.

Pull the Loop Through

Pull the hooked yarn loop through the point where you inserted the hook.

You should now have three loops on the hook.

Yarn Over and Draw the Yarn Through Again

Wrap the yarn over your hook again, then draw it through the two loops closest to the end of the hook.

Draw the Yarn Through the Last Two Loops

You should now have two loops on the hook.

Wrap the yarn over the hook again and draw it through the remaining loops on the hook.

Get Ready to Make Another Double Crochet

With one loop left on the hook, the double crochet is complete. As you practice this stitch, you should start to notice a rhythm to the stitch. In fact, the steps almost blend together so that hooking the yarn over and pulling it through the loops become a single motion: Yarn over and insert, yarn over and draw through, yarn over and draw through.

What you see in the photo above is a turning chain, which counts as a double crochet at the beginning of a row, with the first double crochet next to it.

Each pattern you work should have instructions for what size turning chain to make. Typically, however, you should chain 3 at the start of a row. These three chain stitches create about the same height as a double crochet.

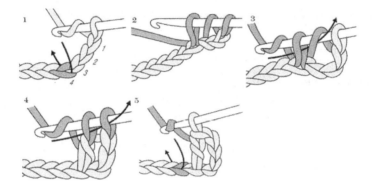

Keep Practicing Your Double Crochet

The more you practice this stitch, the easier it gets. Your stitches should look even and work up faster. Try making a little swatch for practice and to see how it works up!

Tips

The best way to practice the double crochet stitch is by working a straight row of double crochet stitches. Insert the crochet hook below the two loops beneath the stitch in which you are working.

If you're making a granny square or another pattern that uses spaces, insert your hook into the space below the stitch you are working instead of working into the loops. It is a good idea to practice first working in traditional rows and then learning how to work into spaces.

When you work patterns in the future, keep in mind that the pattern might call for you to work a double crochet stitch into a space or into a different stitch. There are many possible double crochet variations, but the basics of the stitch are always the same. What you learn when working in rows will help you throughout all double crochet projects.

5. Half Double Crochet

Half double crochet is a beautiful crochet stitch; it's simple but versatile. It is one of the basic crochet stitches that a beginner should master when learning how to crochet. As the name suggests, HDC is taller than single crochet but shorter than double crochet. It is a foundational crochet stitch and worked similarly to those two basic stitches. A slight difference creates a unique third loop and the smaller height.

Crochet a Foundation Chain

All crochet projects begin with a slip knot.

Next, make a foundation chain to work the first row into. You can crochet a foundation chain, also known as a starting chain, of any length. If you are working with a crochet pattern, use the chain length specified in that pattern.

Start in the Correct Chain

To work the first half double crochet into the foundation chain you will crochet into the chain that is three chains away from your hook.

When you crochet in rows, you begin the row with a turning chain. The height of the turning chain depends on the height of the crochet stitch. In half double crochet, chain two for a turning chain.

Yarn Over and Insert the Crochet Hook

It's time to make the first HDC. Yarn over and insert the crochet hook into the stitch.

Tip. Note that if you were making a double crochet stitch, you would also do this step. If you were making a single crochet stitch, you would not yarn over before inserting the crochet hook. The yarn over adds the height to the stitch, making it taller than the single crochet.

Yarn Over and Pull Through the Stitch

Yarn over again and pull the yarn through the stitch. You should now have three loops on the hook.

Yarn Over and Pull Through the Loops

Yarn over one more time and pull the yarn through all three loops.

That completes the first half double crochet stitch.

Complete The Row

Repeat the steps for each HDC, working across the row of foundation chain and across all the stitches of each subsequent row.

Half Double Crochet Summary:

- Yarn over and insert hook into next stitch.
- Yarn over and pull through.
- Yarn over and pull through all three loops on hook.

To begin the new row, turn the work, chain two for a turning chain. Make HDC stitches in the next stitch and all the following stitches from the row before.

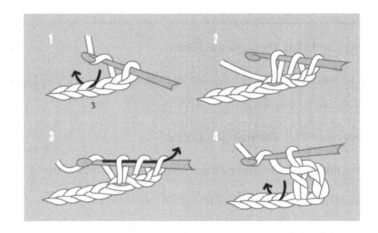

Increasing and Decreasing in Half Double Crochet

With the basic half double crochet stitch, you can crochet any HDC pattern that's worked in consistent rows. But for patterns with shaping, you may need to know how to increase and decrease in half double crochet. Don't worry; it's easy.

How to Increase HDC

To increase, all you do is make an extra half double crochet stitch where you've already made one. Crochet patterns tell you how or where to do this. For example, to increase at the end of the row, crochet two HDC stitches in the final stitch instead of just the one you would usually work.

How to Decrease HDC

Decreasing is a little different, but still easy.

- Yarn over and insert hook into stitch. (as normal)
- Yarn over and pull through. (as normal)
- Yarn over and insert hook into the next stitch.
- Yarn over and pull through. (five loops on the hook as shown above)
- Yarn over and pull through all five loops.

The decrease stitch works over two subsequent stitches to bring the two stitches together at the top into one stitch. You might see it abbreviated as hdc2tog (half double crochet two together) or dec hdc (decrease half double crochet).

6. Treble Crochet

The treble crochet stitch is an important basic crochet stitch that you're likely to need for working various crochet patterns. It is also called triple crochet. It is similar to a double crochet stitch, but slightly taller in height.

Like every other basic stitch, trebles can be combined with other stitches to make interesting stitch patterns. They can be used in a variety of different ways and worked into many different configurations, including rows, squares, circles, triangles, and other shapes.

Begin by crocheting a starting chain. Remember how to work a chain stitch? To work the treble crochet stitch in rows, you'll begin the work by crocheting a series of chain stitches.

Alternately, there are other ways you can get started; for example, you could crochet your treble stitches directly into fabric. Or you could work them into a piece that you've already begun. If that's what you want to do, you'll skip the starting chain and proceed working your treble crochet into the next stitch to be worked.

The first four of your chain stitches will count as your first treble crochet stitch.

When you crochet your next stitch, you'll want to work into the fifth chain from your crochet hook.

Wrap the Yarn Over Your Crochet Hook Two Times

To begin crocheting the next treble crochet stitch, take your yarn and wrap it two times over your crochet hook. There will be three loops on the hook all together, including the active loop you already had. Check out the photo at left to see how this looks.

Work Into the Fifth Chain

You're going to skip the first four chains from your hook (since those count as the first treble crochet stitch); you'll insert your hook into the fifth chain stitch. In the photo at the left, you can see the head of the crochet hook right beside the spot where you will insert the hook to work the stitch.

Treble Crochet Stitch in Progress - Grabbing Yarn

Next, grab the yarn with your hook. In other words, yarn over.

Treble Crochet Stitch in Progress - Pulling Through

Now, pull it through the chain stitch. Steps six and seven together are commonly called, "yarn over, pull through."

Four Loops on the Crochet Hook

You'll end up with four loops on your crochet hook at this point in the work.

Treble Crochet Stitch in Progress - Wrapping Yard

Wrap the yarn around your hook again, repeating step six and pull it through the first two of the loops on your hook. Note that you're only pulling through two loops, which you will be accustomed to doing if you have previously learned how to work a double crochet stitch.

You'll end up with three loops left on the hook. As you'll notice, each time that you do the steps to complete the stitch, you will have one fewer loop on the hook then you did before.

Treble Crochet Stitch in Progress - Wrapping

Wrap the yarn around your hook again and pull it through the next 2 loops on the hook. In other words, repeat steps six and seven again.

You'll be left with two loops still remaining on the crochet hook. You should be getting the hang of this stitch's construction by now.

Wrap the yarn over the crochet hook again and pull it through the remaining two loops on your hook. In other words, complete the stitch by repeating steps six and seven one final time.

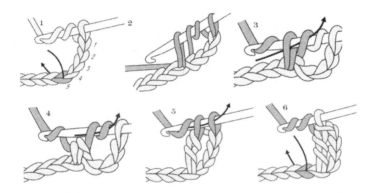

A Row of Treble Crochet Stitches

You'll keep repeating the steps above, over and over again, to make one complete treble crochet stitch in each of the chain stitches in your starting chain.

When you've crocheted across the entire row, here's how the completed row of treble crochet stitches might look.

Crochet Your Turning Chain

The next step is to work your turning chain. The turning chain for a treble crochet stitch is usually 4 stitches, meaning that you will work 4 chain stitches in between each of your rows of treble crochet stitch.

This number of chains isn't set in stone; it's simply a suggested number of chain stitches that works well for a majority of crocheters under ordinary circumstances. There might be plenty of reasons why you'd want to work a longer or shorter turning chain, and you should feel free to do so if you like.

Of course, if your crochet pattern indicates that you should use a different number for the starting chain, then you should follow the pattern's instructions.

Turning the Work

The next step is to work back across the row of treble crochet stitches, building your new row on top of the old row of stitches. To accomplish this goal, you'll have to turn your work over to the other side.

Another Treble Crochet Stitch

You'll work another treble crochet stitch into the top of the stitch you worked in the previous row. Wrap the yarn around the hook twice, insert your hook under both loops of the stitch underneath it in the previous row, wrap your yarn around again, pull it through, and then keep pulling loops through two at a time until your stitch is completed.

From here on out, you can just keep repeating those steps ad infinitum until the piece is as long as you want it to be.

Of course, as with other basic crochet stitches, you can work treble crochet into one loop only (front loop or back loop) to achieve different design effects. If your crochet pattern doesn't state otherwise then you will work through both loops.

Treble Crochet Stitch Worked in Rows

When you are finished, end off by cutting the yarn (leaving a long tail for weaving ends in.) Then pull the cut tail of yarn through the active loop and give it a good tug. Then you can weave your ends in if you like.

At left, you can feast your eyes on a photo of the finished treble crochet stitch fabric.

Essential Beginner Tips

Once you've practiced your stitches, it's time to start working on your own crochet projects. Below is a list of the top ten beginner tips and tricks for you to follow to help you out in your crochet endeavors.

1. Keep your hands clean: You want to avoid getting dirt and grease on your yarn, so wash your hands before sitting down to work.

2. Take frequent rest/stretch breaks: When working through a pattern, it's easy to get lost in concentration and end up holding your yarn or crochet hook too tightly. Stopping to stretch will let you relax your fingers and your back and will help to prevent tired and achy muscles.

3. Keep your crochet necessities in one spot: Keeping all of your yarn, patterns and notions in one place will save you valuable time. You don't want to get tired or annoyed looking for your tools before you even get started, do you?

4. Read through the pattern: Give the pattern you're planning to work on a once-over to make sure you understand what it says and how to do everything. This is also the best time to pop over to YouTube or to check out various crochet video tutorials as needed to brush up on your skills.

5. Check your gauge: Save time and frustration later by taking the time to work up a crochet swatch and check your gauge. Otherwise, your work might end up smaller or larger than intended.

6. Keep your tension consistent: This is a tie-in to the above tip, but try and focus on keeping your tension consistent. This will help you keep your gauge right and steady as well.

7. Don't be afraid to try a different brand of hooks: Crochet hooks are made of different materials and there are even some that are specifically made to be as ergonomic as possible. Look around!

8. Save a small bit of scrap from your project: Once you're done, it might be helpful to save a bit of the yarn you used in case you need to make any repairs down the road, or in case you want to replicate your project.

9. Stitch markers are your friends: When working on a project, whether in rows

or in rounds, use a stitch marker to denote the last stitch of every row or round. This will help you keep track of your stitches and make sure you're following along correctly. For projects that are worked flat, this will also help you keep your edges straight.

10. Block your work: When you're all done with your work, follow our handy blocking tutorial to set your work in place and smooth out any unintentional wrinkles or uneven ends.

11. Don't give up! If a stitch or a project just isn't coming together, keep working on it. Practice makes perfect!

Do's and Don'ts of Crochet

1. DO familiarize yourself with the basics

Take some time to learn about what you need to crochet (just a ball of yarn and a corresponding hook) and how to hold a crochet hook. There's a standard "correct" way to hold a hook, but everyone has their own variation. Experiment and find the position that's the most comfortable for you.

2. DO take time to learn about yarn.

Depending on the project you're making, you might prefer lace-weight yarn instead of worsted weight, or you might want pearl cotton instead of a wool blend. Be sure to read about the standard yarn types to learn more.

3. DO know how to choose your hook wisely.

Crochet hooks correspond with different yarn weights, so what you'll need depends on what you want to make. As you might expect, chunkier yarn needs bigger hooks, and lacier yarn needs the smallest ones. There's also the question of crochet hook type - do you prefer plastic hooks or bamboo? Or maybe you like working with aluminum.

4. DO learn the standard crochet abbreviations.

When you're reading a crochet pattern for the first time, you might be confused by all of the abbreviations. Take the time to know the basic ones, or keep a list handy, like the ones below, to use as a reference guide

CROCHET ABBREVIATIONS

ALT - alternate
APPROX- approximately
BEG - begin/beginning
BET - between
BL/BLO - back loop/back loop only
BO - bobble
BP – back post
BPDC - back post double crochet
BPDTR- back post double treble crochet
BPHDC - back post half double crochet
BPSC - back post single crochet
BPTR - back post treble crochet
CC - contrast color
CH - chain

LP - loop
M - marker
MC - main color
PAT - pattern
PC - popcorn stitch
PM - place marker
PREV - previous
PS/PUFF - puff stitch
REM - remaining
RND(S) - round(s)
REP- repeat
RS - right side
SC - single crochet
SH - shell

5. DO learn the basic stitches.

No matter how complicated the finished pattern might look, it can most likely be broken down into the most basic of crochet stitches: the chain stitch, single crochet, double and half double crochet and treble crochet. Everything else is placement and technique.

6. DON'T get cocky.

Once you know how to crochet the basic stitches, don't immediately jump into an intricate lace pattern. Like in all things, you have to walk before you run. Work up a few smaller, simple projects (think scarves or hats) with basic stitches before moving onto more stylistic crochet stitches and designs.

7. DON'T start a pattern before practicing a new stitch

Practice makes perfect - this is true for all things. Read through how to work a stitch, watch a few videos to visualize it and work up a swatch to make sure you understand how to crochet it.

10. DO know how to care for your finished pieces.

Once you're done with your project, you'll want to treat it well so it lasts and lasts. Depending on the type of yarn you used, you'll need to take care of it differently. Certain yarn can be machine washed and dried while others are far more delicate and can only be hand washed.

11. DO take the time to weave in all your ends.

Weaving in your ends gives your final piece a more finished and polished look - you'll be glad you did! Weaving in your ends is extremely important in the overall quality and hold of your new crochet project over time.